Supercharge Your Productivity

A Small Business Owner's Guide to Getting Things Done, Increasing Profits, and Reducing Stress

By Chaiwat Theerasong

Your Free Gift

To thank you for purchasing *Supercharge Your Productivity*, I created a free worksheet to help you put this book's concepts into action.

Getting results is all about taking action, so here's the link to download your copy of the worksheet:

http://www.chaiwatspace.com/worksheet

Table of Content

Introduction

What does "being productive" mean?

You probably hear this term all the time. Everyone wants to be more productive. Everyone wants to do more. Everyone wants to improve their output.

But what does being productive actually mean? Does going to work make you productive? How about replying to your emails?

Are you productive if you generate money? What if your pay stays the same no matter how much you produce?

The use of the term "productive" invites many rhetorical questions, but most people think productivity is simply the act of moving around or doing something. Here's the big surprise: Work does not equal results.

In other words, just because you put forth effort doesn't necessarily mean you'll get what you want. Work is just work. In many cases, it's a resource used to accomplish a particular goal. Unless you direct your work toward something that matters, it's wasted effort.

You get 24 hours in a day. You usually spend eight hours sleeping, four hours on entertainment, and four hours on activities such as eating and commuting to and from your workplace. This leaves you with eight hours for work. You can invest these hours in a $10-per-hour activity, or you can invest them in a $100-per-hour activity.

A salesperson might have to choose between using his time to reply to emails and using it to make sales calls. If the salesperson is lucky, replying to emails may generate $50 in revenue. Making 100 sales calls can bring in $500 to $1,000 in revenue, depending on the price of the product and the number of people who place an order.

Do you see the difference?

Being productive—actually productive—means doing the things that produce the greatest return on the amount of effort invested. Being productive is making a conscious choice to focus on what's truly important and give up activities that are simply "nice to do."

Being productive is about setting priorities. Now, I'm not talking about categorizing every task as low priority, medium priority, or high priority. Doing that is obsessive, and you'll probably end up with 99 high-priority tasks and one medium-priority task, making it impossible to stay on track. When you have a lot of stuff to do, everything seems urgent and, therefore, everything seems important.

I'm talking about developing a mindset that allows you to determine what's truly important and what's not. To choose to go for a run rather than watching TV. To choose hard, but rewarding, tasks instead of trivial tasks; reading a good book rather than watching a movie—or completing a major task instead of spending hours replying to emails.

This is actually very hard to do.

It's hard because it's difficult to differentiate between what's urgent and what's important. A missed call from your boss is urgent; the task you're working on is important. Email seems urgent, so it takes our attention away from more important tasks. Making 15 sales calls to bring in revenue is almost always a better use of your time than checking email. Every interruption seems urgent. So what are the kinds of work that truly matter?

Being productive is about focusing on the right things. We live in a world full of distractions and interruptions, so it's easy for something to pull us away from important tasks. One minute you're reading messages from your friends; the next, you're reading a blog post, watching YouTube videos, or checking your email. The cycle starts all over again, and before you know it, you've lost one or two hours of work time.

These are just a few of the obstacles that keep you from being productive. If you continue approaching your work the same way, you're going to get the same results, so it's important that you "unlearn" bad habits, figure out what doesn't work, and apply new strategies to increase productivity and maximize your efforts.

In business, the more productive you are, the more profitable you're likely to be. You've probably noticed that successful people seem to be more productive than those who don't succeed in their fields. That's because successful people use specific strategies to accomplish more than others. As a result, there's a strong correlation between income and productivity.

Being productive is about living a balanced life. Do you want to have more time to do what you want? To take your kids to the movies, read a new book, plan the perfect date night, host a party, or earn a new degree? That's cool. But none of these things can happen if you feel so trapped by your work life that you don't have any time for fun.

This book outlines the principles successful people use to stay productive and become high achievers. Your lifestyle may not be the same as everyone else's, but the principles work the same way for everyone. If you apply these principles in your life, I believe you'll achieve success.

With a world full of productivity and management books, why should you read this book in particular? Because there are always opportunities to learn something new and improve your life. I truly believe that reading this book will help you learn how to increase your output without sacrificing the things you enjoy.

Before you tackle the strategies in this book, I want to debunk some of the most common myths surrounding the topic of productivity.

Myth #1: Being productive is about working more hours.

Being productive isn't about putting in more hours; it's about increasing your output. You don't have to work more than eight hours per day if you want to be more productive, but you do need to focus your energy on the tasks that are most important to you. You have about two to four hours per day when your energy is at its highest level. During these hours, you need to be able to focus on the task without allowing any interruptions. Being productive is all about how you allocate your energy.

"There is never enough time to do everything you have to do," says Brian Tracy in his popular book, *Eat That Frog*. Even though there isn't enough time and energy to do everything, the good news is you have enough of both to do the activities that are most important to you. This book will help you learn how to leverage your efforts so that you can multiply your results without working more hours.

Myth #2: Being productive is about doing as much as you can in the shortest amount of time.

Many people tend to multi-task so they can complete several tasks as fast as possible, resulting in a lot of errors. Multi-tasking can also deplete your energy level much faster than normal, leaving you with very little time to focus on important tasks. Later in this book, you'll learn why multi-tasking is one of the worst strategies you can use to get things done. You'll also learn how to get involved with one task at a time. Getting involved with a task allows you to stay focused, be more creative, and produce better results.

Myth #3: You need to be serious at all times if you want to succeed.

Do you think you have to be serious in order to achieve success? For example, do you believe you're not serious about your work unless you work more than eight hours per day, go to sleep later each night, or get frequent headaches?

My program doesn't ask you to do any of these things. Yes, you need to be serious about your work, especially if you tend to procrastinate or have trouble staying motivated. But if you're overly serious, you're going to have problems. Happy people tend to achieve better results, have more creative ideas, and do less procrastinating than people who feel stressed out and overwhelmed. It's better to deal with problems head-on than it is to try to be serious all the time.

I didn't create a fixed system that you have to follow step-by-step. Different people have different characteristics and preferences, so there's no system that works for every single person. In this book, I present sound principles and tell you why they work. Once you understand these concepts, you can easily create a customized system to suit your preferences and lifestyle.

In the end, productivity is about working smarter, not harder. You can work yourself to the bone without seeing results, or you can leverage the strategies in this book to help you accomplish more while having more time to enjoy life.

Who should read this book?

If you run your own business or work from home, you'll get a lot out of this book. I've operated my own business for years, so I've had to go through a lot of trial and error to develop a system that works for me. In *Supercharge Your Productivity,* I share my biggest discoveries so that you can come up with a system that helps you to do more.

However, you can still get a lot out of this book even if you have a full-time job. The tips and strategies in this book are especially helpful if you want to start your own business during your free time. You'll learn how to maximize your time so you can grow your business even while you're working full-time for someone else.

How to read this book

Each chapter of this book contains principles and concepts that act as building blocks for the next chapter. Therefore, I recommend reading this book from the beginning right to the very last page. Once you have a basic understanding of all the principles, you can switch between chapters, as needed.

Some chapters also have exercises to help you learn how to apply important principles. I recommend you take the time to do these exercises, or else you might not get the results you desire. Take as long as you need to complete each exercise. You can also download a free worksheet that complements the concepts outlined in this book. Download the worksheet here:

http://www.chaiwatspace.com/worksheet

Technology plays a big role in our lives, so some chapters have recommendations for mobile apps and online tools you can use to implement each concept. Being productive isn't about downloading dozens of apps, so I only included the tools I think are essential for your success. Before you use these tools, you really need to understand how each principle works.

Please note that most of the strategies in this book are not brand-new breakthroughs. I didn't reinvent the wheel when I was testing new concepts and gathering information. What's different about this book is that I took the time to find out which strategies work for the greatest number of people. I also determined why these strategies work and why other strategies don't seem to help. Then, I presented the information in my own way, along with helpful examples to help you become a master of productivity.

After you finish reading this book, I believe you'll see things in a new light. With a new approach to productivity, you should be able to get more things done than you ever imagined. You'll also feel less overwhelmed and have more time to enjoy your life. In fact, I'm confident you'll see results the very first time you apply one of the principles outlined in *Supercharge Your Productivity*. Enjoy!

Chaiwat Theerasong

Chapter 1: The Mechanics of Success

"Success is nothing more than a few simple disciplines, practiced every day."—Jim Rohn

What is the goal of being productive? Most people want to get more things done, be more profitable, and have more free time, but at the end of the day, we all want to succeed. That's why it's important for you to understand what it takes to succeed before you dive into learning strategies to increase your productivity. This book isn't solely to help you become more productive; it's also to help you enjoy success because of your efforts. The next three principles will help you appreciate the process of work and motivate you to reach your goals. Remember that even the most productive people can fall short on the journey to success if they don't understand the underlying principles.

Principle #1: Think Big

Everything starts with your mindset. You tend to attract the things you think about most often, whether they're big or small. Small goals tend to yield small results, so there's no point in learning productivity strategies if you aren't willing to think big.

What do Donald Trump, Richard Branson, Steve Jobs, Bill Gates, and other successful people have in common? They think big—bigger than most people do.

When you start to think bigger, life gets more exciting. Your journey will take you on a new path that allows you to generate bigger and better results. Howard Hughes, who was one of the wealthiest people in the world, once said, "I intend to be the richest man in the world." With this mindset, he enjoyed being a business tycoon, an aviator, a filmmaker, and an inventor. He made big films such as *The Racket, Hell's Angels, Scarface,* and *The Outlaw* from the mid-1920s to the mid-1950s. Hughes also formed an aircraft company and set multiple world air-speed records.

While reading several books Donald Trump wrote, I learned that one of the reasons he is so successful is because he always thinks big. He also teaches people to think big—way outside their comfort zones, in many cases. This is my favorite quote by Donald Trump: "I like thinking big. If you're going to be thinking anything, you might as well think big."

Richard Branson is also a good example of a successful person who thinks big. His first business venture was a magazine called *Student*, and he didn't stop there. He wanted to live up to his full potential, so he entered the music business by starting a mail-order record company, a chain of record stores, and a record label. After years of success in the music business, Branson entered the airline industry. The Virgin Group now consists of more than 400 companies. In *Losing My Virginity*, Branson said, "My interest in life comes from setting myself huge, apparently unachievable challenges and trying to rise above them."

By giving you these examples, I'm not asking you to set a goal of being a billionaire, but I want to encourage you to think big. Get outside your comfort zone so your life will be more exciting. Daymond John, a multimillionaire entrepreneur known for his clothing line, FUBU, and his appearance on the reality show *Shark Tank*, says, "It takes the same energy to think small as it does to think big. So dream big and think bigger."

There are additional advantages to doing this exercise. When you think big, you get a boost of motivation you wouldn't get if you thought small. Let's say I promised to give you $500 to write a 10,000-word book in one month, but I will give you $10,000 dollars if you can write a 30,000-word book in the same amount of time. Which option would you pick? I think you would pick the second option. When you think big, you're more motivated to succeed, even if the task is more complex.

Thinking big allows you to grow and motivates you to learn new things. For example, imagine you're a salesperson who has worked at the same company for a long time. At one point, you decide you want to be one of the top five salespeople of the year. You draw up a plan to make a certain number of sales calls, read a stack of sales-related books, and attend training seminars to learn techniques that will help you build rapport with prospects. You start using these strengths at work and frequently ask your boss for feedback. As a result, you gain more knowledge and experience. Eventually, you can make more sales than the other salespeople in your company. At the end of the year, the company names you the top salesperson and promotes you to a better position.

Even though this is just an example, it illustrates the benefits of thinking big. If you didn't have a big goal—becoming one of the top salespeople in your company—you wouldn't feel motivated to learn new things. Without growth, you're lucky to maintain your current job in the company and avoid your boss firing you. When you change the way you think, you also change your behavior.

Another advantage of thinking big is that it can lead you to meet like-minded people or people who have already achieved some of your goals. These high-level connections can open doors to bigger, better opportunities.

In later chapters, you will set some goals for yourself. If you already have goals in mind, evaluate them. Do you think you can make any of them a little bigger? If so, this is an exciting opportunity to set bigger goals.

Principle #2: Think Big, Go Small

What prevents you from thinking big? There are two possible reasons: Either you're afraid of hard work, or you think it's impossible to achieve a big goal. It's natural for people to stay in their comfort zones.

The truth is that big goals don't always require big effort, at least not as big as you might think. There's an old saying that applies here. "How do you eat an elephant? One bite at a time." If you focus on the entire elephant, you'll feel discouraged because it's so big. But if you slice the elephant into small pieces (break down your project into smaller tasks), which you can tackle one bite at a time, you should feel more comfortable tackling even the most complex tasks. Thinking big and going small is the way you set goals and approach every project. When you understand this concept, you'll look at your work in a whole new way.

Principle #3: Be Consistent

The key to achieving success is to focus on small actions every single day until you reach your goal. What separates successful people from unsuccessful people is consistency. Successful people understand the power of taking action on a daily basis.

Have you ever heard of kaizen? It's a Japanese word that means "change for better." It's a practice of continuous improvement Toyota and other big companies use. One of the principles of kaizen is that big results come from small changes accumulated over time. You can also apply this concept to your personal life. In simple terms, small changes or small actions plus consistency can produce extraordinary results. If I asked you to take a simple action such as reading 10 pages of a book each day, you would read 18,250 pages in five years! On the other hand, if I asked you to read 18,250 pages, you'd probably think it was impossible. The thought of reading 18,250 pages straight seems as daunting as eating an entire elephant.

Consistency is always the key to achieving success. If you want to lose weight, you can't follow a diet for a few days and then go back to eating junk food. You have to be consistent in your efforts to produce a noticeable result. If you want to write a book, you need to write every day. You probably won't finish your book if you don't write on a consistent basis.

For instance, when Richard Branson started his record label, Virgin Music, his priority was signing new bands. Even though he had a big hit when he signed a contract with Mike Oldfield, it still took him almost 10 years before he could say the business was a success. This was the result of his consistent effort that led him to sign several artists who later became successful such as Human League, Heaven 17, Simple Minds, Boy George, Phil Collins, China Crisis, and Japan.

Success Takes Time

I believe many people fail to achieve their goals because it takes so long to see results. If you quit before the magic happens, you'll never succeed.

Before you pursue any goal, you have to understand that results might not happen very quickly on the journey to success. No matter how much you increase your productivity, it still takes time to achieve your goals. There's no such thing as an overnight success, but there are things such as consistency and discipline. The sad truth is that many people quit before they start to see any results from their efforts. Donald Trump says that most people only see the results of his work, but they don't see how hard he has to work day in and day out.

Don't Give Up!

Think and Grow Rich by Napoleon Hill includes the story of R.U. Darby, a man who tried to dig for gold in Colorado. In the Gold Rush days, Darby's uncle had gold fever. After weeks of hard work, the uncle found a vein of ore, but he needed machinery to bring the ore to the surface. He covered up the vein, went home to raise money from his relatives and neighbors, and finally purchased the equipment.

When Darby and his uncle returned to the mining site, the vein of gold ore had disappeared! They kept drilling, but they didn't find any gold. The men decided to quit and sell the machinery for a few hundred dollars to a junk man.

After Darby and his uncle returned home, the junk man—who was very smart—called in a mining engineer to perform some calculations. The engineer determined that the vein of gold ore was actually three feet from where Darby and his uncle stopped digging! The wise junk man made millions of dollars on the gold he found.

If you ever feel like giving up on your goal, be consistent. If you're sure you're doing the right thing, don't give up before you see results. You may be just a few feet away from reaching proverbial gold.

It's often hard to predict whether your efforts will pay off, but the only way to ensure success is to be consistent in your efforts.

A Momentum Point

If you feel discouraged by your efforts because you're not seeing results yet, look at the illustration below.

Figure 1. How results will compound over time with consistent effort

The illustration shows that your results amplify at a certain point of your effort. Darren Hardy (the author of *The Compound Effect*) refers to this phenomenon as the compound effect. Extraordinary results usually do not happen right away when you start integrating new choices and behaviors into your life. At this point, the results seem intangible. But as long as you're consistent with these new choices and behaviors, over time, the results will compound. The same behavior that you've been doing will give you bigger rewards. At this point, your success will speed up.

Gary Keller (the author of *The One Thing*) explains this concept as a domino effect. One single domino can topple many others, and each domino is capable of bringing down a domino one-and-a-half times its size. When you line enough of them, you can unleash a chain reaction of surprising power.

Think of each domino as your effort. When you start out, the results might happen so slowly that you don't notice, but as you continue bringing down one domino after another with your consistent effort, over time, eventually you'll be moving too fast to stop.

As you can see from this illustration, you shouldn't blame yourself if you're not seeing big results. You might be at the starting point or in middle of the graph, but that doesn't mean you're not taking important steps toward your goals. You must believe that results will come if you continue to be consistent. Track your current results so you'll know whether you're heading in the right direction. If you're not, you can make adjustments and stay on the path to success.

"The harder I work, the luckier I get. When you have momentum going, play the momentum."—Donald Trump

Once you understand the mechanics of success, you're ready to learn several strategies designed to help you get more things done in less time. Although there's no shortcut to success, you can use these strategies to make significant progress toward reaching your goals.

Key Takeaway Points

- You can make your life much more exciting by starting to think bigger.

- Big goals don't require big effort. This game is about tackling one small task at a time.

- Small actions + consistency + time = success

- Don't give up just because you face a temporary defeat. You might be three feet away from gold.

- Your results will compound over time with consistent effort.

Chapter 2: Identify Your Real Priority—The Key to Working Less and Achieving More

"The Principle of Priority states (a) you must know the difference between what is urgent and what is important, and (b) you must do what's important first."—Steven Pressfield

In the next four chapters, you'll learn strategies you can use to develop your own system for being more productive. These strategies will totally change your business game.

Why do you need a system?

Think of system as a framework or process that affects how you approach your work. For your system to produce results, you need to follow it regularly. Doing a morning routine is an example of a system. So is putting in six hours of work each day, exercising three times per week, choosing your activities, or taking breaks. You do these things regularly to keep your system running smoothly.

Systems are supposed to help you focus on things that maximize your efforts. Without a system to guide you, it's easy to veer off the path to success. Life always gets in the way, but following a system can help you focus on the process of getting things done, which is actually the best use of your time. If you always stay focused on results, it's hard to stay motivated and follow through on your goals.

There will be times you encounter a roadblock that shakes your confidence about one of your goals. If this happens, you need to trust that you will get results if you follow the system and continue doing what you're supposed to be doing. Your system "keeps the ball rolling," regardless of what happens in your life.

Using a system also makes it easier to keep the big picture in the back of your mind. This gives you the motivation you need to keep working on projects when things get tough. Do you think Tim Ferriss, Donald Trump, and Tony Robbins use systems to help them succeed? You bet. Their systems might be different from yours, but that's not important. What's important is that each entrepreneur's system generates results.

In this lesson, you'll learn how to develop your own system for increasing productivity and achieving success. Once you understand these principles, you can use them to create a system that suits your lifestyle.

The 80/20 Rule

The first principle of increasing your productivity is learning to understand which tasks are important and which are not.

In the early 1900s, Italian economist Vilfredo Pareto, observed that roughly 20 percent of the people controlled or owned 80 percent of the wealth. He also observed that similar phenomena occur in fields such as science, business, and economics. He eventually established the 80/20 rule, or the Pareto Principle, which states that, for many events, roughly 80 percent of the effects come from 20 percent of the causes. This principle can apply to business in several ways:

- Eighty percent of your sales comes from 20 percent of your clients.

- Eighty percent of your sales comes from 20 percent of your products.

- Eighty percent of your sales comes from 20 percent of your salespeople.

- Eighty percent of the work is completed by 20 percent of your team.

- Eighty percent of your results comes from 20 percent of your efforts.

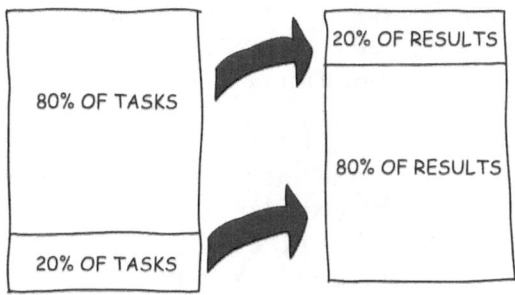

Figure 2. 80 percent of results comes from 20 percent of the tasks.

When you understand this rule, you will realize that the tasks on your to-do list do not have equal levels of importance. Only a few tasks will yield the majority of the results in your business—they're your most important tasks (MITs). If you want to get more results from your work, you need to identify your MITs and spend most of your time on them.

Note that the relationship between your MITs and your results may not be exactly 80/20. Depending on your line of work, your MITs might account for anywhere for 70 to 90 percent of your results. In most cases, the relationship is much closer to 80/20 than 50/50.

The 80/20 rule allows you to increase productivity while working fewer hours because you only focus on the essentials. For example, imagine you own a company that sells five products, and you allocate equal amounts of time and energy to each product. Later, you find out that one of those products generated 80 percent of the sales for your business. What would you do to improve your company's profits? One smart strategy would be to eliminate the product lines that aren't selling well. Applying this strategy reduces the amount of work you have to do, giving you more time to focus on your most profitable product.

Why To-Do Lists Don't Work

A to-do list is supposed to serve as a reminder of all the tasks you need to complete, so using this type of list is one of the most common approaches to increasing productivity. The problem with a to-do list, however, is it doesn't tell you which tasks are the most important. It just gives you a list of tasks to complete. It's possible to check off every task on your to-do list without actually being productive.

By integrating the 80/20 rule into your system, you're going to use a productivity list instead of a regular to-do list. A productivity list is a list comprised of your MITs, or the tasks that yield the most results. Your productivity list shouldn't have hundreds of activities to cross off; instead, it lists a few of your most important tasks. After you complete the tasks on your productivity list, other tasks might not be relevant anymore. If you use a productivity list instead of a to-do list, you're going to get more results in less time.

Purpose and Priority

High achievers understand which tasks are more important than others. They also understand the following:

- Which tasks produce the most results

- Which tasks they should tackle first

- Which tasks to save for later

In other words, high achievers understand their priorities and allocate most of their time and energy to tackling those priorities. This is how you should approach your life.

When you don't have priorities, everything seems important: reading emails from customers, taking a call from your partner, writing a blog post, meeting with your team, contacting potential buyers—the list goes on. That's why you hear people complain about having too much to do, feeling overwhelmed, and not being able to reach their goals. When you identify your priorities early on, it's easy to focus on important tasks and ignore distractions. Most importantly, identifying your priorities reduces stress and helps you accomplish your goals much more quickly.

Before you can identify your priorities, you need to understand your purpose. If you don't know your destination and understand why you want to get there, it's easy to get distracted at any time. Now, you don't need to search for the meaning of life or figure out your ultimate life purpose, but you do need to identify some of the goals you want to accomplish. These goals represent your current purpose.

For example, do you want to make more money? Do you want to learn new skills? Do you want to write a book? Do you want to build a website? Why are these goals important to you? Once you identify your current purpose, you'll be able to set priorities and have a better understanding of what you can do with your time.

Goal Setting

Every achievement starts with a goal. Think of a goal as a target you aim all your effort at, giving you a sense of purpose and inspiration that will remain in the back of your head at all times. Everything you do should align with your goals, and a goal should remind you of what's important and help you get back on track when you stray off the path to success.

Before you read on, set goals for yourself.

Pull out a piece of paper and write down all the goals you have in mind. To give you some ideas, here are six areas of life in which you can set goals: business/career, finances, family, education, health, and spiritual wellbeing.

After you have a list of goals on paper, I want you to pick the three most important goals from the list. These are the goals that you will spend most of your time pursuing right now. I understand that all of your goals are important, but you can't pursue every goal at the same time, or you'll become overwhelmed with everything you have to do. Once you accomplish one goal, you can pursue another one.

Now, make these goals more compelling by using the SMART goal-setting framework. SMART stands for:

S - Specific

A compelling goal should be specific. Compare these two goals: "I will try to lose weight" versus "I will lose 10 pounds in eight weeks." Do you see the difference? The more specific your goals are, the more empowered you feel to achieve them.

M - Measurable

Measurable goals allow you to track your progress over time. For example, the goal of losing 10 pounds in eight weeks is measurable because you can weigh yourself each week and see whether you're making progress. If your goals are measurable, you're more likely to stay motivated.

A - Attainable

Earlier in this book, there were several reasons why you should think big. There's nothing wrong with shooting for the moon as long as it's realistic. Do you have the time and resources necessary to pursue a particular goal? If not, you should adjust your expectations. You can always set a bigger goal once you've reached a smaller milestone. One success will give you the resources and capabilities you need to go to the next level.

R - Relevant

You need to have a good reason why you want to reach your goal. Your "why" is a sense of purpose that motivates you to succeed. If you have a mission, your goal should align with it. Ask yourself whether achieving a goal will really help you to achieve your overall mission or objective.

T - Time-bound

Meaningful deadlines encourage you to take action; therefore, SMART goals must have realistic time frames attached to them. Set a reasonable deadline for achieving each goal but don't give yourself so much time that you start to procrastinate.

This framework is necessary for creating effective goals. Once you have three SMART goals in mind, write them down and post the paper somewhere you're likely to see it often. Every time you see your list of goals, you'll remember why you're working so hard.

Identify Your Priorities

Once you define your purpose by setting goals, you're ready to identify your priorities. This is the most exciting step.

I already told you why knowing your priorities is important: If you want to be productive, you need to focus on your priorities before anything else. You can't tackle every single thing life throws at you— you have to pick the tasks that align with your goals.

The first step in identifying your priorities is to make a list of all the tasks/activities you have to complete to reach your goals. Doing this will help you see the big picture. Then take a deep breath, read the entire list, and put a checkmark next to the most important activities.

Identifying your priorities requires making a realistic assessment of your goals. Priorities are not the things you feel like doing or the things everyone else is doing; they're the tasks that will help you move toward the completion of a goal. Do not choose priorities based on what you enjoy doing or what's easy to do. Instead, choose priorities based on what's truly necessary to achieve your goals.

Note: Please keep this activity list close to you because you're going to use it in the next chapter. You'll learn how to organize these tasks in a way that will make your life much easier. In later chapters, you'll also understand how to delegate and outsource some tasks so you have more time to focus on important activities.

Your priority list should contain approximately 10 to 20 percent of all the activities on your general task list. Every item should contribute to growth and significant results. If you have trouble identifying your priorities, ask what Gary Keller calls the focusing question: *Is this the ONE THING I can do, such that by doing it everything else will be easier or unnecessary?* This question will help you identify your most important tasks and filter out the rest. Take as much time as you need to identify your priorities. When you finish, you'll have a success list to focus on.

The Productivity Pyramid

Aside from asking the focusing question, you can also use the Productivity Pyramid, developed by legendary Internet marketer Eben Pagan to help you identify your priorities.

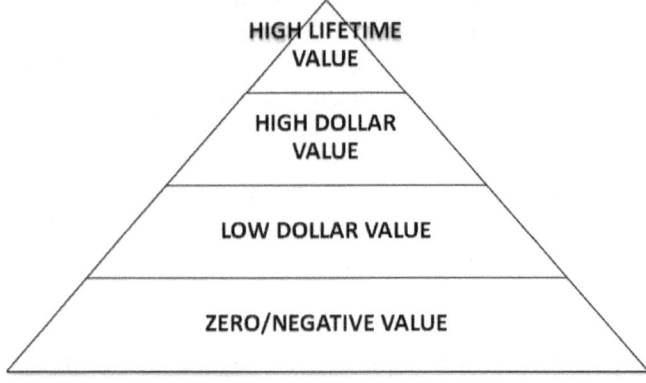

Figure 3. The Productivity Pyramid

The pyramid categorizes your tasks into four levels. Here are explanations:

1. High Lifetime Value

At the top of pyramid are high lifetime value activities. It's the smallest part on the pyramid because it comprises only a few important activities. The nature of these activities is important but not urgent. They contribute to your long-term success if you put consistent effort into them.

In business, these activities would include developing new products and services, building a brand, and creating a marketing plan. In your personal life, these activities include exercising and eating healthy foods.

2. High Dollar Value

At the next level from the top, it's high dollar value activities. These activities bring in results quickly. For example, answering your prospective buyer's questions is a high dollar value activity because if it results in sales, you're going to bring in money quickly.

3. Low Dollar Value

On the third level from the top are low dollar value activities. These tasks generate low results. Most of these are administrative and "busy work" tasks, like organizing papers, packing products, and updating spreadsheets.

4. Zero/Negative Value

At the bottom level is zero or negative value. These activities will waste your time and bring no value or even have a negative impact on your life and business. Examples include eating junk foods, complaining, and worrying.

Ideally, the best use of your time is to spend it on tasks that have high lifetime value and high dollar value. These are your priorities.

To be a master of productivity, you need to identify your true priorities. There will always be new tasks that pop up and force you to quickly decide whether they're important or not. If you're overwhelmed, ask yourself the focusing question or use the Productivity Pyramid framework. This will help you see the big picture more clearly.

If you can't identify your priorities, try modeling yourself after successful people who have reached the same goals. Look for role models who are transparent about what they've done to make a big impact in their industries. Learn their strategies for success by asking questions or reading their blogs or books. As you gain more experience in your role, you will naturally improve at identifying your priorities.

It's natural for your priorities to shift from time to time. We're living in a world where things constantly change. Your business model might change, technology might change, the skill required to do something successfully might change, or your sales might drop. Prepare yourself for these inevitable changes by reviewing your goals every one to three months to see if you need to adjust anything. Reviewing your goals frequently will keep you moving in the right direction.

You now have a productivity list filled with activities that will help you produce big results. Your job is to focus on these activities every day until you reach your goals. Don't change your priorities simply because you feel like doing something else or because something else seems more urgent. We already covered the power of consistency, so keep taking consistent action. Your priorities must always come first.

Key Takeaway Points

- Not all work is equal. Only a few activities yield the majority of your results.

- The key to being productive is to allocate most of your time and energy to your priority list.

- To understand your priorities, you must understand your purpose.

Supercharge Your Productivity

Chapter 3: Getting More Results by Using Your Strengths to the Fullest

*"Over the years, I've learned that a confident person doesn't concentrate or focus on their weaknesses—they maximize their strengths." —*Joyce Meyer

We all have different strengths and weaknesses. I believe that most people spend much of their time and energy trying to succeed in areas that aren't natural strengths for them. At some point, many of these people realize how difficult it is to overcome their weaknesses.

Our environment is a big influence that leads us in the wrong direction. We've learned that the way to succeed is to concentrate on our weakest areas and try to overcome them. As a result, we devote a lot of time, energy, and effort to overcoming weaknesses, leaving our strengths virtually untapped.

In my country, Thailand, students often do tutorials to improve their scores. If I didn't do well in a particular subject when I was in high school, my parents would tell me to study more or send me to tutorials to improve my scores in that subject. Even though my scores always stood out in math, chemistry, and physics, my parents didn't celebrate my strengths. They told me to spend more time studying the subjects I didn't like or excel in.

You have probably been to at least one or two job interviews in your life. What did interviewers ask you? Instead of focusing on your strengths, they probably asked you to talk about your weaknesses. And when you started working, your manager identified your weakest areas in your annual performance reviews, telling you to improve in those areas before your next assessment. Some employees never even get the opportunity to take on roles that match their strengths.

When you socialize with your friends, it's common to hear people talking about the shortcomings of others. Consequently, most of us have tried to improve upon our weaknesses so we feel like society accepts us.

To be more productive, we have to unlearn the conventional way of doing things and apply new strategies to generate new results. Why go against the tide by doing something that isn't natural or enjoyable for you? How can you be productive when you constantly feel frustrated? Productive people are willing to stop doing things that don't work for them; this is something you should be doing, too.

Gallup, a company that specializes in researching the attitudes and behavior of employees, customers, students, and citizens in general, found that people who work on their strengths every day are _six times more likely_ to feel engaged in their jobs and more than *three times* as likely to report having happier lives in general.

Here are more advantages of using your strengths:

- You'll be happier and have more satisfaction.

- You'll be engaged in work and have more focus.

- You'll learn new information and approaches faster.

- You'll enjoy doing your work.

- You'll feel a greater sense of accomplishment.

In *Now, Discover Your Strengths,* Marcus Buckingham explains that you can never change your core talents. Your mental network (the way your brain cells connect) formed during the first few years after you were born. He says that the configuration of your mental network, with its range of stronger to weaker connections, doesn't change much after your mid-teens.

This tells you that you shouldn't waste your time trying to change your talents. They don't change. Instead, you should accept your natural talents and turn them into strengths you can apply in your field. This way, you can maximize your efforts and multiply the results you get from your work. If you look at the people around you, you see that those who live their lives with passion are playing to their strengths.

Right now, your challenge is to identify your strengths and weaknesses so you can start working to improve your strengths. This is a powerful way to increase your productivity.

How to Find Your Strengths

So, the question is how you can identify your strengths. Finding them isn't easy, but it's not that hard either. You have to observe your own behavior, stay in tune with your feelings, and listen to feedback from others. Here are three effective ways to help you discover your strengths.

1. Observe your own behavior.

The first step is to think back to your past, particularly those experiences you had at a young age, and identify the activities that excited you. What activities did you really enjoy? When you were excited or loved to do something, you were most likely using your natural strengths. Write these activities on a piece of paper and determine why you enjoyed each one. For example, do you want to feel significant? Do you love competitions? Do you like to be around other people? The answers will give you some clues about your innate talents.

While you do this activity, notice how you approach each task. In a situation that uses your strengths, you will typically stand out from the crowd. Make note of any events where you outperformed other people; then ask yourself why you did so well.

Another area you have to assess is your ability to learn something new. If you can learn something very quickly, it might be one of your natural talents.

Once you've completed this step, you should also list the activities you hated to do in the past, and figure out why you hated them. Doing so will help you uncover some of your weaknesses. Later on in this chapter, you'll find strategies to manage around your weaknesses.

2. Listen to feedback from your friends, family members, and colleagues.

Getting feedback from other people is a great way to discover your strengths, so make a list of three to four friends you can trust to give you honest feedback. Ask each person to tell a story about a time when you performed at your peak. Then ask the following questions:

- What activities do I do best?

- What makes you think I'm good at those particular activities?

- What are my unique qualities?

- What are my strengths and talents?

You might want to record each person's answer so you can listen to it in detail later.

3. Use tools designed to help you identify your strengths.

Several online strengths tests will help to evaluate your skills. I've tried many of them, and I found that the Clifton StrengthsFinder, developed by Gallup scientists, gave the best insights. It will identify your five dominant talents from the 34 different areas in the StrengthsFinder database. It takes around 30 minutes to complete the test. When you finish, you'll receive a report that lists your strengths and gives you some strategies for taking advantage of them.

Access this test by visiting the Gallup Strengths Center online (https://www.gallupstrengthscenter.com). The price of the evaluation is $9.99. You can also buy Tom Rath's book, *Strengths Finder 2.0,* which contains an online access code for the test. The test is well worth your time and money.

If you don't want to spend any money, use the strength assessment tool from the University of Kent, which has 52 short questions. Here's the link:

http://www.kent.ac.uk/careers/Choosing/strengths.htm

This site uses your answers to give you a score for 13 key attributes. The larger numbers are your strengths; maximize them. Here's the link:

How to Use Your Strengths to Your Advantage

After you've discovered your strengths, it's time to map out a plan for using them. In the previous chapter, you identified your priorities. Now, think about specific ways to use your strengths to work your way through the priority list you created. This will help you leverage your talents so you can produce more without working extra hours. After your complete this step, you will reach a productivity level that only a few people can master.

Here's a worksheet to help you track your strengths and use them to your advantage.

Strength #1: _____

Characteristics of this strength:

_____
_____ .

Strategies for leveraging this strength in my work:

_____

_____.

Disadvantages associated with this strength:

_____

_____.

Ways to improve this strength:

_____

_____.

To access a PDF version of this worksheet, and to print out the worksheets from other chapters, visit this page:

http://www.chaiwatspace.com/worksheet

The reason you should write down the disadvantages of each strength is that there are times your strengths can cause problems you don't see coming. For example, I'm a very focused person; I need to be efficient and stay on track. Even though this strength has helped me make progress toward my goals, the flip side of this strength is that I'm impatient with delays and obstacles, and I'm not always sensitive to the feeling of others since I want to accomplish my priorities.

When you're aware of the problems that might arise from using your strengths, you can lessen the impact they have on you. In my case, when I understand the negative side of my talent, I try to be more patient with delays and obstacles, and I make sure that I give some thought to other people's feelings.

It's not enough to maximize your strengths in your work; you also need to work on improving them. The more you improve your strengths, the more advantages you will have in your field. That's why you wrote down some ideas for gaining more knowledge and skills. (You did, didn't you?) You might need to go to seminars, watch video courses, read books, or even ask for advice from successful people in your industry.

How to Manage Around Weaknesses

Now you understand that focusing on improving your weaknesses isn't the best use of your time. Focusing solely on weaknesses prevents failure, but it's not the best way to achieve extraordinary results. But does that mean you have to totally ignore your weaknesses? No.

Weaknesses act as roadblocks, so it's helpful to know the areas that you have less talent in. When you see potential problems, you can work to minimize the impact they have on your life.

Here are three strategies to help you mange around your weaknesses:

1. Stop doing the activity that weakens you.

When you do something that doesn't use your strengths, ask yourself whether the activity is even necessary. Can you stop doing it or, at the very least, spend less time on it? If so, start doing activities that help you focus on your strengths.

2. Get a little better (good enough) at it.

If your role requires a certain talent you lack, it can undermine your strengths and make you question your abilities. The solution is to try to improve on your weakness just enough to do your work and focus on your strengths. Remember that you can't turn weaknesses into strengths no matter how hard you try.

3. Partner with other people.

Getting help from someone who excels in one of your areas of weakness is the best way to manage around your weaknesses. By using this strategy, you'll have more time to focus on activities that use your talents, and the other person can use his or her talents to produce quality results.

When you start using your strengths and stop focusing on your weaknesses, your life will improve immensely. You'll love your work and be more productive. If you unknowingly spend time trying to turn your weaknesses into strengths, you will never achieve extraordinary results, and you'll have a hard time with your work. It's important to do the exercises in this chapter so you can focus on your strengths and stop doing what isn't natural for you.

Start using your strengths today.

Key Takeaway Points

- Working on your strengths is the key to staying fully involved in your work, having more satisfaction, and increasing productivity.

- Keep improving your strengths so that you'll have more advantages in your field.

- Don't try to turn your weaknesses into strengths. They don't change.

Chapter 4: Developing a Personal Productivity System for Completing Tasks

"Your mind is for having ideas, not holding them."—David Allen

One trait productive people have in common is that they always seem to know the right action to take at any given moment. They don't let their ideas overwhelm them or cause confusion about what they should do. Productive people use systems to help them identify what's most important right now and then determine what to do next. If you want to be a productive person, you need to develop your own system for organizing and categorizing ideas.

Trying to remember things—the email you have to send, the article you need to write, the assignment you need to give your assistant, the call you have to make, or the new idea that might boost sales—robs you of your productivity. When you have too many ideas running around inside your head, it's easy to get confused about where to start. You might even forget what you have to do next. Our brains aren't supposed to carry these ideas all day long, so you need a workable system for capturing ideas and figuring out what you need to do with them.

The system in this book is based on David Allen's, the author of *Getting Things Done*. You might have seen his full system before, but this is a simplified version that's still very effective. If you've already read *Getting Things Done,* you might have found Allen's system to be a little overwhelming, especially for beginners. I want to give you a system that yields results without overwhelming you.

Using this system has several benefits:

- Your will have an organized life.

- You won't have to struggle to remember everything.

- The ideas that pop into your head during the day won't overwhelm you.

- Your focus on your work is stronger.

- You won't have to worry about what you should do next.

To use this system effectively, there are three principles you need to follow.

1. Capturing

The first step in putting this system to work is having a safe place to capture your ideas, whether they're new tasks, project ideas, or random thoughts that pop up suddenly. If you don't capture these thoughts and get them out of your mind, you'll have to keep reminding yourself of your ideas. This is not a good way to use your brainpower. In addition, these thoughts can distract you when you're trying to focus on work.

Figure 4. Whenever you have new ideas pop up, get them out of your mind right away.

The safe place where you will put all of your ideas is an inbox. You can put this process to work by using a small notebook you carry with you at all times, or you can use a note-taking app on your smartphone. This way, you can capture ideas as soon as they pop up, and you won't have to worry about forgetting anything important. Make it a habit to capture your ideas right away.

2. Processing

The second step is processing your inbox. You will usually tackle this step at the end of the day. To process each item in your inbox, look at the list below and make a quick decision about what you need to do. There are typically five things you can do with an item:

- **Add it to an action-item list.** The action-item list tells you what you need to do next. If you use this list, you won't have to waste time wondering what you should do. Just look at the list, and you'll know right away what you should focus on.

- **Add it to a delegation list:** The tasks on your delegation list are the tasks you plan to outsource or delegate to others. For help deciding which activities to delegate, read the chapter titled "Get More Done and Increase Profits by Outsourcing."

- **Add it to a to-do-later list:** Any task you need to complete in the future should go on this list. When you add a new task, give it a deadline and add it to your calendar so you don't forget about it. These tasks will be your priority tasks in the future.

- **Keep it for reference:** Some items won't be actionable right away, but you don't want to forget about them. For example, you might have some ideas for the name of a new product you're developing. You'll keep these ideas in a reference folder so you can easily access them in the future. You might need to create different file names or categories of reference for each project to eliminate confusion.

- **Trash it:** When you review your inbox, you might find that some of your ideas are not as important as you thought they were. Delete these ideas or put them in a trash folder.

Project Lists

You can feel overwhelmed when you see a long list of tasks that you create. Instead of having one long list, you should create lists for different projects; for example, I have project lists for each book I'm writing, a project list for my business, a project list for my blog, and project lists for my email marketing and advertising campaigns. Using project lists makes it easier to see the big picture of each project.

When you're processing your inbox, you need to assign each item to an appropriate project list. Let's say I have these five items in my inbox:

- Film an advertising video

- Write an article about the benefits of tea

- Call Jane

- Design a logo for my blog

- Do market research

Assume that I've already created three project lists: @Blog, @Advertising Campaign, and @Product Development. Here's an example of how I would process my inbox:

Item	What to Do	Project List
Film an advertising video	Delegate	@Advertising Campaign
Write an article about the benefits of tea	Defer(Date: mm/dd/yy)	@Blog
Call Jane	Action item	@Advertising Campaign
Design a logo for my blog	Delegate	@Blog
Do market research	Action item	@Product Development

As you can see, processing your inbox helps you avoid feeling overwhelmed by the running list of tasks in your mind. The system tells you what you need to do, how you need to do it, and when you need to do it for every item in your inbox. As a result, you don't have to worry about forgetting important tasks or ideas. Processing your inbox also frees up your mind so you can focus on the work in front of you.

If you don't empty your inbox regularly, it's easy to feel overwhelmed by everything you need to do. Try to process your inbox at least once per day, if not more often.

Now it's time for an exercise to help you understand the concepts we just covered.

Exercise

In the previous chapters, you were supposed to write down all the activities you needed to complete to accomplish your goals. Think of this step as the capturing process. The paper you used to write down each activity was your temporary inbox.

Right now, apply the concepts from this chapter by processing all of your activities. Make a quick decision about what you should do with each activity and then assign each item to a project list. If you've already identified your priorities, then you've already taken the first steps in processing your inbox. If a priority requires immediate action, add it to your action-item list. If you don't need to complete a task until a future date, add the task to your to-do-later list.

Trash or add to your delegation list those tasks that don't fit in either category. After you complete this exercise, you should have a thorough understanding of how to use this system.

Tools Needed

Now that you understand the mechanics of the system, here are the tools you need to put it into action.

1. A small notebook for collecting ideas, tasks, and projects. I recommend using a notepad that's small enough to carry with you at all times.

2. A calendar for scheduling all your tasks. When you move tasks from your inbox to your to-do-later list, you need to assign a deadline for completing each task.

3. A sheet of paper to write down your action items. These items are your priorities for the day. Keep this paper close to you at all times so you can easily identify your next task.

4. A three-ring binder to create project lists for each project. My project list @Blog would have two items: Write an article about the benefits of tea (defer), and design a logo for my blog (delegate). Put all related documents, ideas, and task lists in this binder.

The Digital Approach

Smartphones have become a big part of our lives. These days, people use their phones to check email, surf the Internet, send messages, jot down ideas, and so on. Smartphones are very popular, and there are several apps that can help you easily implement the concepts in this chapter.

This is the best time to describe these apps because you needed to read about the concepts behind them first. Now that you understand the principles of productivity, it's a good time to learn how to use your smartphone to increase your output.

If you don't like using smartphones or other digital devices, there's nothing wrong with using traditional tools such as notebooks and three-ring binders. You can also create a blended approach by using a smartphone for some tasks and a notebook for other tasks.

Here's a list of apps I found helpful for creating a personalized productivity system.

App #1: Evernote (Free, $2.99/month, $5.99/month)

Evernote is an all-in-one note-taking app that makes it easy to capture ideas. This tool captures and stores everything from text-based notes to images and allows you to organize them in a way that's easy to access. Evernote syncs to the Web, desktop software, and a smartphone app, so you never have to worry about losing important information.

There are many ways to use Evernote to increase productivity. For example, I can use Evernote to capture emails I want to read later. My approach is simple. If an email comes in while I'm busy with my work, I just forward the email to my Evernote email account. The email is stored in Evernote until I'm ready to read it, so I don't have to worry about forgetting to read any of my messages. If you sign up for Evernote, you'll receive an Evernote email when you register your account.

You can also use Evernote to do the following:

- Clip interesting web pages so you can read them later

- Capture ideas by taking pictures of paper documents

- Take notes while reading books and magazines

Evernote offers three pricing options based on usage: Basic (Free), Plus ($2.99/month), and Premium ($5.99/month). Here's some detail on the three pricing options:

https://evernote.com/pricing/

App #2: Nozbe (30-day free trial; $10/month)

Nozbe has transformed the way I manage projects. A productivity expert, *Michael Hyatt*, also uses and recommends this app. I've been using the app for more than a year, and I really like it. It's a task-management app based on the Getting Things Done methodology, so it's a perfect fit for the concepts in this chapter. The main purpose of Nozbe is to capture tasks and project ideas. Once you capture an idea, you turn it into an actionable to-do item.

What I like about the app is that I can easily create project lists, and it allows me to assign context for each task I create, such as @home, @computer, @errands, @waiting for. For each task you add to Nozbe, you can create notes, attach files, set a priority, and schedule time to work on the task. Nozbe also connects with popular tools such as Evernote, Google Calendar, and Dropbox. As you can see, Nozbe does a lot of the heavy lifting for you, making your life a lot easier.

Here's the link: https://nozbe.com

App #3: Wunderlist (free, $4.99/month)

Wunderlist works pretty much the same way as Nozbe. What I like about this app is that you can add subtasks for each to-do item. This makes it easier to organize tasks. For the paid version ($4.99/month), you can add unlimited subtasks and upload files of any size.

For individual tasks you add to Wunderlist, you can also add a note, images, or your note voice, and import Dropbox files. The main disadvantage of this app compared to Nozbe is that it doesn't connect with Google Calendar and Evernote. That's why I prefer to use Nozbe.

Visit Wunderlist website by following this link below:

https://www.wunderlist.com

Note: Pricing information and app features are accurate as of the publication date of this book. By the time you read this, app prices and features may have changed.

Tip: If you don't want to spend money on Nozbe or Wunderlist, use Evernote instead. It's less convenient, but you can make it work with the concepts in this book. If you decide to use Evernote, create notes that represent an inbox, next actions, and individual projects to help you manage your ideas.

Look at the image below to see what I mean.

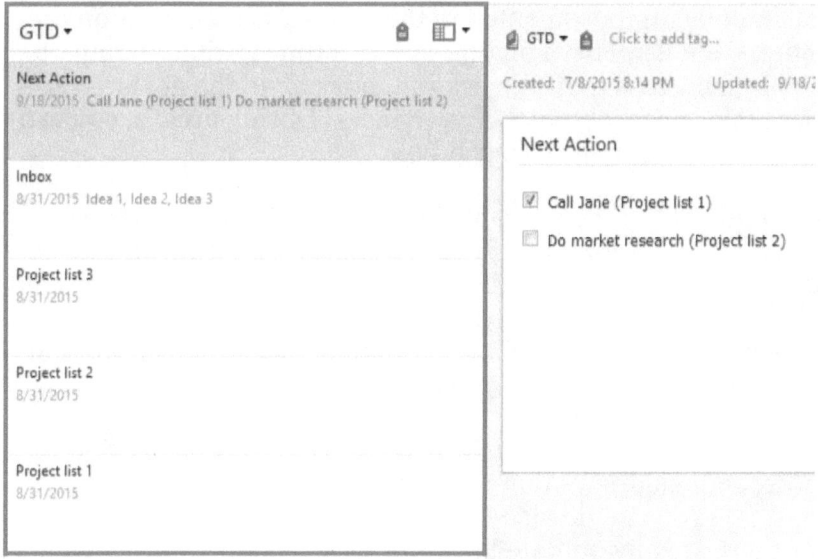

Figure 5. You can use Evernote to make the GTD methodology work for you.

App #4: Google Calendar (Free)

Google Calendar is a Web application and mobile app created by Google. It's better that you mainly use the Web version on your laptop rather than your smartphone, for two reasons. First, with the Web version, your calendar and schedule display on a larger screen. This makes it easier to see the big picture and understand how tasks and due dates connect. Second, it's easier to create and manage tasks on the Web version than it is on the mobile version.

One thing I like about Google Calendar is that it can be set up to automatically sync with the calendar app that came with your smartphone. If you work on team projects, you can also share your calendar with your team members so everyone can see what you're doing at any given time.

Here's the link to access Goggle Calendar:

https://www.google.com/calendar/

3. Doing

The last and most important step in this system is taking action on your action-item list. Focus on one task at a time until it's complete. After you finish, cross it off the list and move on to the next task. If necessary, take a short break between tasks. During breaks, you can capture new ideas or empty your inbox.

After you understand the concepts in this chapter, try the system and see how it works for you. If you find the system difficult to use, you can make adjustments until you find something that works. Just remember not to procrastinate on putting the system to work for you. Once you have a personalized system in place, you can work at a faster pace without getting overwhelmed.

At least once per week, preferably on Sunday, you should review your inbox and make sure there aren't any tasks you haven't processed yet. You should also review your project lists and see whether there are any outdated tasks or tasks you forgot to cross out once you completed them. Then look at your calendar to see whether there are any tasks from the past week that you need to move forward. Following this 10-minute process each week will help you stay on the right course.

In the next chapter, you'll learn how to maintain your focus, engage with your work, and increase your energy level. Doing these three things will help you become much more productive.

Key Takeaway Points

- Free up your mind by getting everything out of your head. Your brain is ready for fast decision-making, not carrying ideas all day long.

- Make it a habit to process your inbox as least once a day. This way, you'll never have to worry about forgetting to do important tasks.

- Use the benefits of your smartphone to apply the concepts in this chapter.

Chapter 5: How to Stay Focused and Engaged in Your Work

"The first law of success is concentration—to bend all the energies to one point, and to go directly to that point, looking neither to the right or to the left."—William Mathews

This chapter is about how to find your focus when you're working. Many people struggle with a lack of concentration, making it difficult to stay focused and achieve success. We live in a world where distractions are a big part of our lives. Devoting more time to distractions than to important tasks seems perfectly normal. As a result, we've become less productive and less engaged with our work.

Have you ever started a fire by using a magnifying glass? If not, here's how it works. You put some tinder in a certain spot and then hold a magnifying glass at an angle that focuses the sun's light on as small an area as possible. With the right amount of concentration, the tinder starts to smoke and eventually catches fire. This is a perfect example of the power of concentration and focus. When you focus, you don't pay attention to other things—you concentrate your energy on the most important thing in front of you.

You might have had an experience when you were intensely focused and engaged with your work. In your focused state, you probably found it easy to perform your work to a high standard. You may have even enjoyed your work. The key to increasing your productivity is to make sure you're in this focused state more often so that you produce better results. In this chapter, you'll find four strategies to help you get your focus back and increase the level of engagement you experience with your work.

1. Eliminate distractions

Distractions are now a normal part of our lives. Social media, email, text messages, advertisements, online videos, and requests from other people are just a few of the things that can take your attention away from more important tasks. With all these distractions, it's easy to lose your focus at any time.

You might be surprised by the amount of time you waste on distractions. A study done by Basex, a New York research firm, found that office distractions eat up <u>2.1 hours per day</u> for the average worker. If you're self-employed, this number might be much higher, since you don't have anyone keeping track of your behavior. A friend of mine who works from home admitted that, on average, he wastes three to four hours per day on distractions. In your case, the number of hours wasted could be higher or lower, but you have to realize that distractions can eat up a lot of your time. Imagine what you could do if you didn't waste so much of your time on distractions!

When you allow yourself to be distracted for too long, the distraction becomes your main focus. As a producer, you need to eliminate as many distractions as possible. Even if you only eliminate half of the distractions you typically face, you can increase your productivity dramatically. Doing so will give you more time to focus and produce work at a high level.

Here are three effective strategies for eliminating distractions.

1. Track how you spend your time.

The first step in dealing with distractions is to know how you spend your time. Most people try to work while unknowingly allowing distractions to interrupt their focus. In many cases, people don't even realize how much time they've wasted on these distractions. If you notice this pattern in your own life, you have the power to stop it.

Think about a typical day at work. What distractions tend to eat up a lot of your time? When do you usually get distracted? How much time do you spend dealing with distractions? Write your answers on a piece of paper.

Here's an example:

- Responding to text messages and emails after waking up—20 minutes

- Surfing the Internet before starting work—30 minutes

By looking at how you spend your time, you can quickly identify unproductive behavior and take steps to control it in the future.

2. Create a distraction-free environment

A powerful way to eliminate distractions is to create an environment that makes it virtually impossible for you to be distracted. For example, I used to put a smartphone next to my bed to use it as an alarm clock. When I shut off the alarm in the morning, I automatically checked my messages right away. After I realized I was wasting a lot of time on this activity, I decided to place my smartphone far away from my bed and use an old-school alarm clock instead. Making just one change to my environment helped me avoid checking messages first thing in the morning, so I could start working earlier each day.

The best way to create a productive environment depends on your personal situation and preferences. One thing you can do is to turn off all notifications on your smartphone while you're working. It's hard to resist the temptation to read and respond to messages when you see them pop up on your smartphone. If possible, you should also place your smartphone far away from your work area. It'll surprise you how easy it is to focus on work when you aren't tempted to check your phone.

If people tend to interrupt you while you're working, establish some rules about when you're available and let people know in advance. If the situation doesn't improve, consider moving to a different location. This is easier to do if you're self-employed, but if you work for someone else, your boss might let you switch offices if it will help you be more productive.

3. Use time blocks

Using time blocks is another good way to improve your focus. If I told you to work for five hours straight, you might feel overwhelmed and discouraged. When you know you have to work long hours, you might intentionally let distractions get in your way so the time passes quickly. If you have this problem, time blocks are the solution. If you know you just have to be productive for 30 or 60 minutes, it's easier to focus on your work.

The amount of each time block is up to you. Some people feel comfortable working with 60-minute time blocks, while others prefer to focus for 30 minutes and then take a break. If you have a short attention span, try working in 10-minute time blocks. The key to choosing the right interval is trying them all and seeing which one helps you stay focused.

Add some fun to the process by using a system Francesco Cirillo developed—the Pomodoro Technique (http://pomodorotechnique.com). One pomodoro, or tomato, consists of a 25-minute work session followed by a five-minute break. During your 25-minute work session, you need to focus on your work and avoid distractions. Once you set your goals for the day, all you need to do is determine how many "tomatoes" you need to complete for each task.

Apps to Improve Your Focus

There are many apps designed to help you eliminate distractions and boost your focus, but just two apps have been a big help to me.

App #1: RescueTime (Free, $9/month, $72/year)

RescueTime allows you to see how much time you devote to being productive compared to how much time you spend on distractions. As I said earlier, you have to understand your behavior before you have the power to change it. If you see that you spend a lot of time on YouTube, for example, take steps to avoid YouTube and spend more time on work.

One interesting feature of this app is that you can give each of your activities a "productivity rank" based on whether the activity is a productive or distracting use of time. RescueTime uses the data to gauge how productive you are on a scale of 1 to 100. You can also view daily, weekly, monthly, or yearly productivity statistics.

The paid version of RescueTime allows you to do the following:

- Restrict the amount of time you spend on certain websites

- Access more detailed reports

- Get alerts on how you've been spending your time

Here's the link to visit RescueTime website:

https://www.rescuetime.com

App #2: StayFocusd (Free)

The second app is StayFocusd, an extension for Google Chrome that allows you to block access to certain websites. What's good about this extension is that it's easy to customize according to your preferences. You can block or allow certain websites or specific pages, paths, subdomains, or types of page content (videos, photos, games, etc.).

To install StayFocusd, open Google Chrome browser and following this link: https://chrome.google.com/webstore, then type "stayfocusd" on the search box.

App #3: Focus Booster (Free)

A timer is a must-have for productive people. Focus Booster can create time blocks or apply the Pomodoro Technique.

https://www.focusboosterapp.com

2. Stop multitasking.

It's funny to see how many time-management articles there are about mastering multitasking. At one time, multitasking seemed like the best way to get things done fast. The truth is that multitasking is a recipe for disaster.

The important thing is to stay focused and involved with your work. When you switch back and forth between tasks, you're not fully engaged in anything. Research shows that dividing your attention among several tasks pumps you full of adrenaline and stress hormones that affect your brain function over time, reducing your attention span. As you will learn soon enough, multitasking also uses up your energy very quickly.

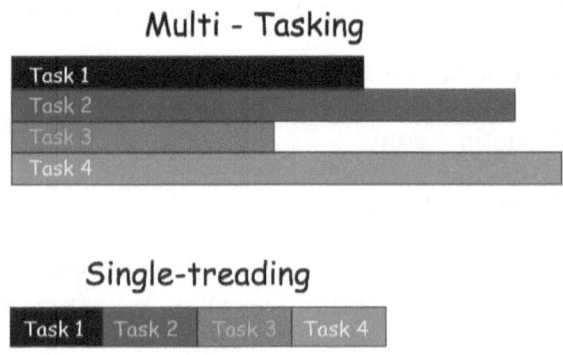

Figure 6. Illustration based on the work of Étienne Garbugli's presentation, "26 Time Management Hacks I Wish I'd Known at 20"

The above illustration shows that you get things done faster when you focus on one thing at a time.

Multitasking merely kills your focus and increases the amount of time it takes you to finish a task. In experiments published in 2001, Joshua Rubinstein, PhD, Jeffrey Evans, PhD, and David Meyer, PhD found that participants lost significant amounts of time as they switched between different tasks. As tasks got more complex, participants lost even more time.

Meyer has said that even brief mental blocks created by shifting between tasks can reduce your productivity as much as 40 percent.

If you want to be productive, eliminate the temptation to work on many tasks at once. Focus on one thing at a time; when you finish, move to another task. This is the best way to focus on your work. Remember that you can't concentrate on everything in every moment.

3. Manage your willpower

Willpower is what you need when you want to focus and engage with your work. It's defined as "the faculty by which a person decides on and initiates action; control deliberately exerted to do something or to restrain one's own impulses." In other words, willpower is the ability to direct yourself to take action and then focus on that action consistently. It's easy to procrastinate if you don't have the willpower to stay on task. If you have willpower, you operate on a different level. You have an easier time focusing, a longer attention span, and the ability to be decisive when it comes to solving problems. Disciplining yourself requires much less effort—that's the magic of willpower.

Willpower is a limited resource.

If you want to increase your willpower, the first step is to understand that willpower is a limited resource. Roy Baumeister conducted an experiment on willpower in the late 1990s. In his study, he placed a plate of warm chocolate chip cookies next to a plate of radishes. He allowed some participants to eat the cookies, while others had to eat only the radishes.

After this test of sheer willpower, participants had up to 30 minutes to solve an unsolvable maze. Participants who had already used up their willpower by eating only radishes and resisting the cookies gave up on solving the maze after only eight minutes. Those who ate the cookies gave up on the maze after an average of 20 minutes. This shows us that the participants tasked with resisting the cookies used up most of their willpower. When it came time to work on the maze, they were too tired to exert any more effort.

Professor Baba Shiv of Stanford University also conducted an interesting study on willpower. Participants in one group had to remember a two-digit number, while participants in the other group had to remember a seven-digit number. Then, the researchers told both groups to walk down the hall and choose one of two snacks: a slice of cake or a piece of fruit. The students who had to remember the seven-digit number were nearly twice as likely to pick cake as the students who had to memorize two digits.

How are these findings relevant to you? As you can see from these experiments, willpower is a finite resource. If you use it to do one thing, you have less of it available for doing something else. You can deplete your willpower even faster if you do any of the following:

Complete a big task. Some activities require more attention and focus than others. The more self-control you need to complete a task, the more willpower you use and the less energy you have left.

Form a new, difficult habit. Forming a new habit depletes your willpower the same way completing a big task does. The more self-control you need to master the habit, the more willpower you use.

Multitasking. Think of your willpower as a laptop battery. If you run multiple programs at once, the battery dies faster. The same thing happens with willpower.

How to Increase Your Willpower

In 2007, Professor Baumeister and his colleagues asked students to perform tasks that required a certain amount of willpower, such as watching a long, boring video. They found that these students had significantly lower blood-sugar levels than students who had to complete simple tasks.

In another experiment, Baumeister assigned students a task requiring a high level of self-control and attention. Then, he asked them to drink a glass of lemonade. Some participants had lemonade with real sugar (buzz) and the others drank lemonade with Splenda (buzzkill). When the students completed their tests of self-control, the second group made twice as many errors as the group that had lemonade made with real sugar.

Baumeister's findings show that, even though you have a limited amount of willpower, you can replenish it when it's gone. It's up to you to manage your willpower and refuel when necessary, so you may need to change your lifestyle if you want to become a high achiever.

Here are four tips to help you increase your willpower and manage it effectively.

1. Eat healthy foods

Baumeister's experiment shows that eating the right foods can help you replenish your energy, so it's important to eat healthy foods throughout the day. Check out this list of healthy foods from Vinchay Labs and see if you can integrate any of them into your lifestyle.

https://vinchaylabs.com/look-great-grocery-list/

2. Tackle your most important tasks at the beginning of the day

You have the highest level of brainpower in the morning, so you should use the beginning of your day to tackle the most important tasks on your priority list. When you have less energy, you can work on easier tasks.

3. Take breaks

Research shows that taking breaks during work helps you replenish your willpower. When you schedule your day, be sure to allocate enough time for breaks.

4. Reduce stress

When you're stressed out, you can't work efficiently because you're using your brainpower to focus on all the stress in your life. This is the energy you want to use for doing your most important tasks. Reduce stress by trying meditation or using other stress-reduction techniques. Many people report that practicing meditation for at least 10 minutes each day helps reduce stress over time.

5. Putting yourself in a resourceful state

In the book *Unlimited Power*, Tony Robbins explains how our internal states affect productivity. Most people spend their time in one of two states: a resourceful state or a paralyzing state. Have you ever worked and felt as if everything seemed to flow because you were centered and focused? You were in a resourceful state. In contrast, being in a paralyzed state is confusing, makes it difficult to engage with your work, and causes a lot of frustration. The good news is that it doesn't matter what state you're in right now. You can transition from a paralyzed state to a resourceful state by doing the exercises below.

How to Change Your State of Mind

If you want to enter a resourceful state, here are two things you need to do.

1. Change the pictures in your mind

How you picture things in your mind affects your internal state. Successful people tend to look at things in ways that empower them to produce results, while unsuccessful people let their circumstances direct their thinking. The first thing you need to do is learn how to picture things in a way that empowers you.

Before you start working on an important project, close your eyes and think about a time when you were in a resourceful state and everything seemed to flow. What pictures did you see in your mind? What were you thinking about? Notice how you felt and try to keep that feeling for as long as possible. When you open your eyes, you should feel more focused and alert. You have shifted into a resourceful state that helps you stay focused and engaged with your work.

2. Shift your posture

A lot of research shows that body language and posture affect your internal state. Erik Peper, professor of health education at San Francisco State University, studied how a change in posture can affect mood. He found that sitting up straight made it easier for participants to conjure up positive thoughts and memories. A related study completed by Ohio State University researchers in 2009 showed that sitting up straight reinforces confidence. Researchers from Columbia University and Harvard University found that open, expansive postures increase feelings of power and an appetite for risk.

Peper also found that skipping during a break can significantly increase energy levels. In contrast, students who had a sad, slumped walk experienced a decrease in their energy levels.

What does all of this mean for you? It means you need to focus on your posture. The correct posture can help you transition into a resourceful state and increase your level of engagement at work. Try to sit up straight and stand up tall. Don't maintain a closed, constricted posture.

Stop reading right now and check out your posture. Are you bending your back and putting your shoulders forward? If so, sit up straight and use a more expansive posture. You'll start to feel better in just a few moments.

When you do these exercises consistently, guess what? They'll become habits! Once you've ingrained these habits in your mind, you can automatically tap into a resourceful state when you start working.

Key Takeaway Points

- Distractions kill your focus and consume a lot of your time. As soon as you stop these distractions, you'll start to become more productive.

- Multitasking is a bad strategy to approach your work. You'll do more and produce better results when you focus on one thing at a time.

- Your willpower has limited resources. It's your responsibility to manage it so you'll have enough of them to tackle your most challenging tasks.

Chapter 6: 7 Essential Habits of Productive People

"The difference between an amateur and a professional is in their habits. An amateur has amateur habits. A professional has professional habits. We can never free ourselves from habit. But we can replace bad habits with good ones."— Steven Pressfield

There's a saying that the majority of your success comes from your daily habits. What you do most frequently dictates the results you produce. We all know that some habits are useful and some are not, so it's important to acknowledge bad habits and try to replace them with new habits that will improve your life.

Think of what your life would be like if you woke up late every day, spent a lot of time surfing the Internet and chatting with friends, ate a lot of junk food, and chilled out with friends five times per week. If you have these habits, you can stop thinking about becoming productive because you won't have enough time and energy to focus on your work.

To achieve a higher level of success, you need to develop productive habits and drop the habits that block you from getting results. Seven habits are essential to achieving a high level of productivity. You might already follow some of these habits; if you do, that's a good thing. Let's see whether there are other habits you can develop so you'll have a greater chance to achieve success.

Here are the seven essential habits you must have if you want to be a productive person.

1. Get quality sleep (seven to eight hours per night)

You've probably had the experience of waking up and feeling exhausted. This is usually the result of not getting enough sleep. Lacking sleep not only makes you feel fuzzy, it also affects the prefrontal cortex, the part of the brain responsible for forethought, judgment, impulse control, and organization. When you're in this state, you can't perform at your peak level. You're also more likely to make mistakes.

Your body and mind need to rest and recharge, but getting fewer than six hours of sleep isn't enough. You need to sleep for at least seven to eight hours per night to wake up feeling refreshed and ready to work. The best way to get enough sleep is to go to bed earlier. We're not programmed to stay up late. If you like to surf the Internet or watch television at night, you need to eliminate these activities so you can get to bed earlier. Have you ever downloaded a TV series to watch and kept watching episode after episode to find out how the show will end? Watching TV and using the Internet late at night can also make it difficult to fall asleep because you're thinking about what you just saw or read.

Getting out of bed earlier can actually boost your energy level in the morning, giving you the boost you need to produce better results. Remember that the early bird catches the worm. When you wake up early, you will have more time to do important things.

App: Sleep Cycle ($0.99)

One problem that makes people feel tired after waking up is that they awaken during their deep sleep phase.

That's where the Sleep Cycle app comes into play. Like an intelligent alarm clock, it tracks your sleep patterns and wakes you during a light sleep phase, which is the optimal time to wake up.

The app works by monitoring your movement (your movements can tell the app what sleeping phase you're in) during sleep using a sensitive accelerometer in your smartphone. Then it will find the optimal time to wake you during a 30-minute window that ends at your set alarm time.

If you have a hard time waking up in the morning or trying to wake up earlier and want to feel rested and relaxed, you can use this app to wake you naturally.

Here's the link to Sleepcycle website:

http://www.sleepcycle.com

2. Don't check your email first thing in the morning

Checking your email and social media accounts first thing in the morning can eat up a lot of your time. Before you know it, you've already wasted one or two hours of your day without accomplishing anything. As we discussed earlier, you will have your highest levels of energy and willpower first thing in the morning. You need to use the first few hours of your day to tackle the complex tasks on your priority list. You can always check your email after you've already completed your morning routine or checked off an important task. If you add up all the time you save by not checking email first thing in the morning, it's possible to save several hundred hours during the course of a year.

3. Eat healthy foods in the morning

Morning is when your body needs the most energy—the right kind of energy. That's why breakfast is the most important meal of the day. The problem is that most people want to eat a quick breakfast, so they eat whatever they have on hand. Unfortunately, most of these foods are processed foods or junk foods. That's why so many people feel the mid-morning slump and struggle with "brain fog": the feeling of a lack of mental clarity and focus, along with confusion and forgetfulness.

A healthy breakfast gives your body the glucose it needs for the brain to function after a night of sleep. Studies also show that eating breakfast can improve memory, boost concentration, and make you feel happier as your stress levels decrease. Healthy breakfast foods provide you with a stable source of energy for the most critical part of your day. If you want to improve your focus and increase your energy level, make a habit of eating healthy foods in the morning.

Ruth Frechman, the author of *The Food Is My Friend Diet,* recommends eating a breakfast that is 25 percent protein, 25 percent carbohydrates, and 50 percent fats. The easiest way to form this habit is to prepare breakfast ingredients ahead of time. If all of your ingredients are ready when you wake up, you have no excuse not to prepare a healthy breakfast.

4. Tackle challenging tasks before lunch

In the last chapter, you read about doing your most challenging tasks in the morning because it's when you have the highest amount of energy. Putting first things first also helps you make real progress toward achieving your goals. If you complete your most important tasks in the morning, you don't have to worry if your energy level declines in the afternoon because you've already had a productive day.

5. Exercise regularly

You may have noticed that most successful people start their days by doing light exercise because it has so many benefits. In *Making a Good Brain Great,* Dr. Daniel Amen writes that anything that's good for your heart is also good for your brain. Exercise increases your heart rate, pumping more oxygen to your brain cells. Research also shows that morning exercise increases your brain activity and prepares you to tackle complex situations during the day ahead.

Regular aerobic exercise, also known as cardio, appears to boost the size of the hippocampus, the area of the brain involved in verbal memory and learning, according to a study led by researchers at the University of British Columbia. Jogging, walking, dancing, cycling, and swimming are all examples of aerobic exercise. Set a goal to do any of these exercises for at least 20 minutes per day, three days per week. Researchers at the University of Georgia found that exercising for about 20 minutes can facilitate information processing and memory functions in the brain. You can even make the process more exciting by listening to your favorite music while you exercise or, in my case, by listening to audiobooks.

6. Read good books

There's no question that reading has many benefits. Books give you the knowledge you need to tackle many of life's challenges. Reading a book is also a good way to improve your focus and reduce stress, because it gives you practice at focusing on one thing at a time.

If you don't enjoy reading, a good way to develop the habit is to set a goal to read a book for just 20 minutes each day. Twenty minutes doesn't seem like a lot of time, but it adds up quickly. If you read for 20 minutes per day, every day of the year, you'll end up reading for a total of 120 hours per year. Just imagine how much knowledge you will gain if you develop this habit. If you already enjoy reading, you might want to set a goal of reading for 45 to 60 minutes per day.

7. Try new things

Another trait successful people seem to have in common is they're willing to try new things. When you take a risk and try something new, you'll get results one way or another. If the risk pays off, you have a new skill or piece of knowledge to use to your advantage. If it doesn't work, at least you had the opportunity to experience something new.

Think of yourself as a scientist. Scientists are always testing new theories to see whether they work. If one theory turns out to be wrong, they keep trying new theories until something finally pays off. If you want to be more productive, don't hesitate to try new things. The reason there are so many exercises in this book is to give you an opportunity to see whether any of these concepts work for you. If something doesn't work, that's okay. At least you're one step closer to finding something that helps you stay focused and productive. Most of the concepts in this book will work for you as long as you put them into practice, but it's okay to make adjustments if a few of them don't fit your lifestyle.

When you learn something new, make a habit of putting it into practice right away. Otherwise, you might forget what you learned.

There you have it: the seven habits of productive people. They're not just tips you should try sometime in the future, they're habits you should practice every day until they become routine. Following these habits consistently will help you produce better results in all areas of your life.

In the next chapter, you will learn how to successfully form these habits. Most people fail to develop new habits because they don't understand how to form them. After you learn the concepts in the next chapter, you'll see that developing new habits isn't as hard as you might think.

Key Takeaway Points

- What you do frequently dictates the results that you get in your life.

- Understand that the habits you're using are the first steps to developing new behavior that allows you to be more productive.

Supercharge Your Productivity

Chapter 7: The Effective Way to Develop New Habits (and Make Them Stick)

"Repetition of the same thought or physical action develops into a habit which, repeated frequently enough, becomes an automatic reflex."—Norman Vincent Peale

You've learned about the habits that can make you more productive. The most challenging part is developing these habits and making them stick. Developing a new habit isn't exactly easy, but it isn't too difficult. In this section, you'll learn how to successfully form new habits.

Understanding Habits

The first step to developing a new habit is to understand how a habit forms. For example, driving a car can eventually turn into a habit.

Most people feel uncomfortable when they drive a car for the first time. You have to focus on the road, stay in control of the vehicle, and watch out for pedestrians, cyclists, animals, and other drivers. What you might not know is that doing something new uses a part of your brain called the prefrontal cortex. The prefrontal cortex needs a lot of brainpower to help you make decisions.

The more you drive, the less your brain will rely on your prefrontal cortex. Instead, it will pass the job to the basal ganglia, the part of your brain responsible for emotions, memories, and pattern recognition. Once your brain stops using the prefrontal cortex, you don't have to use as much of your brainpower. You'll feel comfortable driving, and then driving will become almost automatic. When you reach this state, it's possible to arrive somewhere without really knowing how you got there. In other words, driving a car becomes a habit.

As you can see, a habit forms by consistently repeating a particular behavior over time. The challenging part of developing a new habit happens at the very beginning of the process. It requires some discipline to implement a new behavior consistently, especially if you don't feel like it. As time passes, you don't need as much brainpower to maintain the behavior. One of the main reasons people fail to develop new habits is because they quit before the habit finally sticks.

How long does it take for something to become a habit?

Most self-help experts say it takes 21 days to form a new habit. Researchers from the University College London showed that it takes, on average, 66 days for something to become a habit. Some participants in the study developed new habits in as few as 18 days, but it took others as many as 254 days to make their habits stick.

It doesn't matter how long it takes you to form a new habit. As long as you're consistent, you'll eventually succeed. If you want a good rule of thumb, however, expect to spend about 21 days developing a new habit. If the behavior seems natural to you after 21 days, you can work on developing a new habit.

Following these steps will make it easier for you to develop new habits.

1. Focus on a few habits at a time

Don't set yourself up for your failure by trying to develop several habits at once. There are two reasons why this doesn't work. First, as you learned in previous chapters, implementing a new behavior requires you to use willpower, a limited resource. If you use your willpower for one thing, you won't have enough willpower available for other tasks. If you try to form several habits at the same time, you'll almost certainly fail due to a lack of energy.

Second, the human body craves internal stability, or homeostasis. When you try to develop a new behavior, your body tries to fight it, especially if the change is a big one. Unless you've had a dramatic experience that motivates you to change everything about your life, you probably won't get very far if you try to form several new habits at the same time.

It's much easier to make a few small changes or focus on a few habits at a time. This way, your body won't put up much of a fight against the change, and you won't use up all your willpower. Note that your body will have an easier time adapting to a new behavior if the behavior is easy to implement. For example, getting into the habit of drinking a glass of water when you wake up every day is a lot easier than developing a habit of exercising daily.

When a new behavior becomes something you do automatically, it requires less of your brainpower. Eventually, the behavior becomes a habit. Therefore, developing habits is a sequential process.

Forming new habits is somewhat difficult, but there's some good news. Once you form a new habit, it's easier to develop additional habits. As an example, people who exercise regularly tend to pick healthier foods than people who don't exercise. In *The Power of Habit,* Charles Duhigg says that practicing self-regulation—playing soccer or exercising regularly, for example—can help you gain more discipline in other areas of your life.

Look at the seven habits again. Select one or two of these habits to develop in your own life. Try to pick the habits you think are most important right now. If you don't get enough sleep, for example, getting seven to eight hours of sleep per night will help you.

2. Decide when you're going to implement a new behavior

You already set up a system to help you be productive, so now you need a system to help you form new habits. Build your own system by deciding when you will start implementing a new behavior. For example, "I will wake up at 6:00 every morning for 21 days in a row." A clear plan helps you stay motivated, even when you feel like giving up on your new habit.

3. Identify any obstacles in your way

Write down any obstacles you encounter while trying to develop a new habit. If I want to develop a habit of exercising every day, one obstacle might be my friends asking me to go out during my scheduled exercise time. If I choose to go out with my friends instead of exercising, I have to start the process all over again.

4. Set rewards

Every habit has an inherent reward behind it. If you love to exercise, you might crave the rush of endorphins you get after a run. People who enjoy healthy foods probably expect to enjoy better health or a sense of control over their lives. The problem is that these inherent rewards might not be so obvious when you're first starting out. To stay motivated, you might have to set some tangible rewards. For example, if you love to eat cookies, you might want to reward yourself with a piece of a cookie after an exercise session. The goal of using the cookie as a reward is to get off to a good start. Over time, your brain will start expecting the inherent rewards of exercise and stop craving the cookie.

For some people, long-term rewards are better than short-term ones. If you meet your goal of behaving the same every day for 21 days, you might want to get a big reward to celebrate your success.

5. Find support

Without support from friends, family members, or colleagues, it's difficult to stay motivated. That's why finding support is a powerful way to build a new habit. One way to do this is to ask a friend to hold you accountable. You can even use a punishment approach to shape your behavior. If you don't wake up at 6:00 in the morning, your punishment might be giving your friend $100. Fear of punishment is a powerful motivator, so it's useful for developing hard-to-form habits.

Another way to find support is to join a community of people who are trying to reach the same goal. Feel free to share your goal, ask questions, and answer questions community members post. Participating in this type of community creates a sense of commitment, making it more likely you will stick with the new behavior. It's easy to find a supportive community by using relevant keywords to search Google or Facebook.

App: Coach.me

If you have a smartphone, you can use the Coach.me app to develop new habits. The app is free, and it allows you to track your progress toward achieving your goals. Coach.me also features a supportive community where you can make new friends, ask questions, and share your experiences. One way to stay motivated is to follow people who are trying to reach the same goals you are.

The first time you use Coach.me, you need to pick the habits you want to develop. Every time you successfully implement a behavior, just click the check-in button. The app will show you how many people accomplished that goal on the same day. If you still have trouble staying disciplined, you can even use the app to hire a coach to help you.

https://www.coach.me

You Must Believe

Finally, forming a new habit is to believe in yourself and the process. Nothing can stop the habit-development process except your limiting beliefs. If you believe you can do something, you'll behave in a manner that supports your belief.

Successful people believe in the power of commitment, so you need to be committed to your goals. If you're committed to improving your life, developing new habits will become much easier.

These are the simple steps you need to take to form new habits. One thing you need to remember is that there's no need to rush the process. You don't have to develop hundreds of new habits to succeed. In fact, just one or two of the right habits can improve your life dramatically. Be patient and take as much time as you need.

Key Takeaway Points

- The most challenging part to forming a new habit is at the beginning of the process. If you're consistent with the new behavior, over time, it will become automatic and require less effort.

- Don't set yourself up for failure by trying to develop several habits at once. Start with a few habits that will make the most impact in your life right now.

- Develop a system to use the new behavior consistently by following the five-step process.

Chapter 8: How to Beat Procrastination and Double Your Productivity

"Procrastination is the art of keeping up with yesterday." —Don Marquis

When you're trying to get things done, do you ever fall into one of these situations?

- You plan to do too much, accomplish too little, and get frustrated because it doesn't feel as if you're progressing fast enough.

- You wait until the last minute to muster up the desire to get things done.

- You've found yourself losing focus while working on your priority list, so you end up doing an easier task just so you feel as if you accomplished something.

If you answered "yes" to any of these questions, then you might have a problem with procrastination.

Procrastination is one of the most common problems people face, and it's hard to overcome. You know you should exercise, but you don't. You know it's time to work on an assignment, but you put it off. You know you should be working, but you spend time surfing the Internet instead. When you procrastinate, you know exactly what you should be doing, but you can't motivate yourself to do it. Procrastination is the biggest enemy of productivity. Imagine if you procrastinated for two hours each day, surfing the Internet and watching YouTube videos. You would lose around 700 hours in just one year!

Why Do We Procrastinate?

There are many theories about why we put things off or why we don't do what we should. People procrastinate for three main reasons: a lack of confidence, a lack of energy, or the presence of a psychological issue. In this chapter, you will read a guide to tackling each of these areas and overcoming procrastination.

Lack of Confidence

Lacking confidence and self-esteem is one of the biggest reasons people procrastinate. They say things like:

"I don't know if I'm doing the right thing."

"What if it doesn't work out?"

"I think I'll do that later."

"I don't have enough time for this activity."

"What if other people are doing it better than I am?"

"If I don't make my project perfect, people will see my flaws."

The list goes on.

When you lack self-confidence, your work seems very intimidating. Imagine you're gambling, and you have to put your chips on the table. If you have a pile of 100 chips, you're not afraid to bet 10 of them because you'll have plenty left. But if you have to put down all your chips, you might freeze up because it threatens your sense of security.

Compare that with, say, starting a business. Suppose starting a business takes 100 self-esteem points, but that's all you have. You have too much at stake, which can lead you to procrastinate. Eventually, you might even abandon the idea because you think failure will kill you (it won't). The more you have at stake emotionally, the more likely you are to procrastinate.

People see work as intimidating and risky because they associate their self-worth with their innate abilities. This can create fear in many forms: fear of failure, fear of falling short of perfection, fear of difficulty, and fear of feeling overwhelmed.

Letting criticism damage your self-esteem goes back to your childhood. When your parents criticized you, you were too young to know whether their criticism was reasonable and logical or not. You accepted the criticism at face value and believed that whatever had gone wrong was your fault. This may have contributed to your tendency to procrastinate.

If you can increase your confidence, you will be less likely to put things off. Here are three ways to boost your confidence about work.

1. Break the project into smaller tasks

If you see a project as being big or complicated, it's easy to feel overwhelmed and start procrastinating. Overcome this problem by breaking down every project into a series of smaller tasks. This makes projects seem less complicated and increases your confidence in your ability to get things done. This is how successful people approach their work; they focus on one small action at a time.

2. Reframe the context

If you think your work is complicated, you're more likely to put it off until later. Therefore, you need to change your perspective. It's possible to view your work in a different way by thinking of what you see as a "complication" in a new frame of reference that brings you excitement. If you feel excited about your work, it's easier to start and stay on track. Ask yourself these questions if you need to reframe a complication:

- Is there a step-by-step procedure I can follow?

- Are there small steps I can take to build momentum?

- Can I break this project into a series of simple tasks that I can enjoy doing?

You should also think about a time when you faced a similar challenge. Here's an example:

"When I was in college, doing projects for professors was more difficult than completing this project, but I managed to pass. So why doesn't this project feel easier than that?" Use this technique to counter negative self-talk and reframe the situation. Use the examples to change your perspective and increase your confidence.

3. Start small

One of the best ways to increase your confidence is to work on a task for just 10 to 20 minutes. You'll be surprised when you realize how much your confidence increases after completing one simple task. Starting small validates your ability to tackle the entire project. Usually, people find that tasks are not as difficult as they initially thought.

Whenever you find yourself procrastinating, set a timer for 10 minutes and start working right away. There's no excuse not to work on a project if you only have to work for 10 minutes.

4. Forget perfection

When you attach your self-worth to your performance, you want to do everything perfectly so other people accept you. This gives you far too much to do and makes it easy to feel overwhelmed, causing you to procrastinate when you should be working.

The easiest solution is to forget about striving for perfection and change your state of mind. You can do this by using your imagination. When you're about to start working, imagine yourself as an artist drawing a sketch for a painting, a first draft of sorts. Knowing that you can correct your mistakes later relieves the pressure you're putting on yourself. Without the threat of criticism from yourself or anyone else, your creative juices will flow.

Lack of Energy

If you lack energy, either the mental or physical type, you may feel too tired to do what you need to do. This undermines concentration and often triggers procrastination.

In 2003, Tony Schwartz and Jim Loehr introduced the concept of managing energy. Their book, *The Power of Full Engagement,* says that managing energy, not time, is the key to high performance and personal renewal. They argue that having more energy creates a greater capacity for work. Without good energy management, good time management isn't enough to help you succeed.

Most people lack energy because they eat a lot of junk food, avoid exercise, and don't get enough sleep. In fact, these are three of the most common causes of low energy and procrastination.

If you want to increase your energy level, work on developing the habits described in previous chapters: eating healthy foods, getting enough sleep, and exercising regularly. When you have more energy, you will have a greater capacity for completing important projects. Therefore, you'll be less likely to procrastinate.

Psychological Issues

Brain function affects every aspect of our lives. These days, more people have short attention spans, obsessive-compulsive disorder (OCD), depression, and anxiety. The reason for these problems lies inside the brain.

People with unbalanced brains—that is, brains with some overactive parts and some underactive parts—often have severe problems with procrastination. If a car's engine is faulty, it won't run well even if it has a brand-new transmission. When your brain isn't working right, your mood isn't right. When your mood isn't right, you don't want to work—and you end up procrastinating.

Dr. Amen says:

"Will-driven behavior comes from a healthy brain. It allows you to exert conscious choice over a situation to work in your own best interest. Will-driven behavior is goal-directed and productive; it helps you reach the goals you have set for your life."

If you have a healthy brain, you'll have more willpower and a more positive attitude. Unfortunately, many people have bad habits that impair their brain function.

Dr. Amen uses a method called SPECT (single-photon emission computed tomography) to see activity patterns in the brain. Thousands of SPECT studies show that most people have unbalanced brains. Biological and environmental factors can alter brain function. In today's world, certain factors seem to hold more weight than others.

Repeated thoughts, multitasking, anxiety, and depression have the greatest effect on our brain structure and function.

One way to overcome repeated thoughts is by writing down the ideas running inside your head in a small notebook or note-taking app as mentioned in an earlier chapter. Also, quit multitasking. If you have a problem with anxiety or depression, you need to deal with it right away so it doesn't affect your performance.

To get started, read the article from Lifehack.org. It gives 15 simple tips for overcoming depression and sadness. Here's the link:

http://www.lifehack.org/articles/lifestyle/fifteen-simple-ways-overcome-depression-and-sadness.html

Key Takeaway Points

- Boost your confidence by detaching your self-worth from your ability and performance. The more confidence you have, the less likely you'll procrastinate.

- Increase your energy level by eating healthy foods, getting enough sleep, and exercising. Having sufficient energy allows you to do more work.

- Overcoming repeated thoughts, multitasking, anxiety, and depression can result in healthy brain functioning. A clear mind can help you work in a flow state.

Chapter 9: Get More Done and Increase Profits by Outsourcing

"I think one of my strengths is that I can always take advice, and I can delegate. I know a lot of people feel the need to do everything themselves, but I am not one of them." —Dasha Zhukova

Productive people realize the importance of getting help from others, so they don't attempt to do everything by themselves. They understand the value of their time and know how to limit the amount of time they spend on mundane tasks each day. To get things done, productive people learn how to outsource tasks to other people.

The main goal of outsourcing is to free up time to work on more important tasks. Ask any of the great entrepreneurs, and they will tell you that time is your most important asset. No matter how hard you work, you'll never have enough time to do everything. Outsourcing gives you time to work on important projects and get more enjoyment out of your life.

I know there are some readers who work full-time and want to start their own businesses. If this applies to you, you have less time available than people who are self-employed. This makes outsourcing even more important if you want to be competitive and get things done.

The Advantages of Outsourcing

Imagine there are two guys named Keith and Brian. They are both starting the same type of business—manufacturing and selling wooden watches. The difference between the two is their mindset regarding outsourcing. For some reason, Keith wants to do everything himself, including designing, manufacturing, and marketing the watches. As a result, every task is a priority. He works 10 hours per day and produces 100 watches per month.

Brian has a different mindset. He understands that he can't do everything by himself if he wants his business to flourish. He has the big picture in mind, so he identifies the core of the business and figures out which tasks he can outsource. Brian is good at tasks requiring innovation and creativity, so he decides to focus on designing watches. He outsources research, manufacturing, assembly, packaging, quality control, and marketing tasks to other people. As a result, he works four hours per day and produces 500 watches per month.

These results are just the beginning. After one year passes, Keith is now producing only 80 watches per month because he's bored and exhausted. He can't expand his business, so he decides to shut it down. In contrast, Brian's business is thriving. His company is producing 2,000 watches per month. People are starting to recognize the brand, so he's generating a lot of word-of-mouth publicity. All of this is possible because Brian focused on the core of his business and outsourced the rest. Now he has more time to enjoy life and start other businesses.

This example illustrates the advantages of outsourcing quite well. Brian could produce more watches and have more free time. In other words, he was more productive than Keith. He spent most of his work time on what he excelled at and borrowed the expertise of others to keep the business running. So, you learn how to overcome the obstacles that might prevent you from outsourcing. Also, later in the book, you'll find an outsourcing protocol that can help you maximize the return on your investment.

What prevents leaders from outsourcing?

Even though many people realize outsourcing is a great idea, some obstacles prevent them from doing so. It's important that you overcome these stumbling blocks so you can realize all the benefits of outsourcing business tasks. Here are the five main obstacles that prevent people from outsourcing.

1. The quality is poor

One of the most common concerns associated with outsourcing is the fear that no one else will perform up to your expectations. If you have this mindset, you're likely to take on every task necessary to keep your business running.

To overcome this mindset, you need to create a rule to help you determine when to outsource. John C. Maxwell says that if someone else can do something 80 percent as well as you, delegate it. If you're a student, and you have a term paper to write at the same time you need to clean your house, you can outsource the cleaning to a friend or cleaning service and focus on the term paper. Doing well on the paper is more important than cleaning, and even if no one else cleans as well as you, at least the job gets done.

If you accept 80 percent quality, you can actually cross some tasks off your list. If you expect 100 percent quality at all times, some tasks will never get done because you won't have enough time to do them yourself.

2. I enjoy what I'm doing

If you enjoy what you're doing, you might not want to outsource the task to someone else. This isn't a problem if you're doing the right things, but if you enjoy doing unimportant work, outsourcing is the best option.

To overcome this obstacle, you need to identify your priorities. If you don't know your priorities, everything seems important, and you're likely to do the tasks you most enjoy, even if those tasks have no impact on your long-term success. A few years back, I wanted to create a website sales page to sell gym equipment. Even though I enjoy this type of task, I outsourced it to someone else because I realized I had more important things to do.

3. Doing it myself is cheaper

You might think it's cheaper to do tasks yourself instead of paying someone else to do them for you. This problem usually arises when you don't set goals properly and don't understand what outsourcing can do for your business. Remember, the main advantage of outsourcing is that it gives you more time to focus on your core strengths. If you do everything yourself to save a few bucks, you'll have less time to focus on tasks that can generate more revenue.

4. I don't have time

Now that you know how to save time with outsourcing, you might be surprised that one of the reasons people avoid delegating is because they think they don't have time for it. Carol A. Walker, the president of Prepared to Lead, a leadership consulting firm, says, "Most people will tell you they are too busy to delegate—that it's more efficient for them to just do it themselves."

If you're too busy to outsource, you'll be busier doing the tasks yourself.

You can eliminate the excuse of not having enough time by scheduling the time for outsourcing activities in advance. For example, you might set aside one hour in the afternoon—after you've already finished your most important tasks for the day—to manage or monitor your contractors.

Outsourcing Protocol: A Five-Step Process

Now that you know the advantages of outsourcing and the best way to overcome each of the obstacles preventing you from doing it, you have to get used to outsourcing and delegation. Here's a five-step process to help you use outsourcing effectively.

1. Identify the tasks you plan to delegate

The first step is identifying the tasks you plan to delegate or outsource. Here are three types of tasks you should consider outsourcing.

a. Repetitive Tasks

Repetitive tasks that have a low dollar value consume a lot of time. You should delegate or outsource these to someone else to free up time to scale your business. Examples of repetitive tasks include checking products for manufacturing defects, providing customer service, updating spreadsheets, and packaging products for shipment.

b. Areas That Are Not Your Expertise

If a task requires skills you don't have, outsourcing should be your first choice. If you're not an expert, you're not going to create something spectacular, and you shouldn't spend time trying to develop skills that might take years to master. Get the job done fast by outsourcing it to someone who has a lot of experience.

c. Tasks You Hate to Do

Doing something you don't like drains your willpower, leaving you incapable of tackling other challenges. You should reserve willpower for doing your most important tasks, not the mundane tasks you can outsource to someone else. If you hate building websites, for example, hire someone else to do it.

A quick exercise

In the chapter titled "Identify Your Real Priorities," you wrote down all the tasks required to accomplish your goals. Look at this list again and decide which activities you can delegate by using the criteria outlined above. This is the same approach you will use when processing your inbox.

2. Find a contractor

After you identify the tasks you plan to delegate, the next step is to find the right person to do the job. The first place you want to look for a contractor is to ask friends, family members, or colleagues for recommendations. When someone gives you a referral, ask for an honest opinion of the contractor's work. Three qualities you should look for are quality, speed of delivery, and accountability.

If the people in your network don't have any referrals for you, the next place to look is a freelance marketplace. It's much easier to outsource in the digital age; all you need to do is post a job on one of these websites, and several people will send you their proposals. Here are four services you might want to try:

1. Upwork.com

2. Freelancer.com

3. Guru.com

4. http://jobs.problogger.net

Before you post a job on one of these sites, you have to identify the task you want to outsource, set a budget, develop a project timeline, and determine the skills a freelancer needs to complete the project successfully. Be prepared to share this information with freelancers when you post your job.

Selecting a Contractor

After you post a job on one of these websites, you'll probably get quite a few proposals from freelancers. You should collect proposals for three to four days before you start reviewing them. This gives you the best chance of finding the right person for the job.

Before hiring a freelancer, you need to understand that some contractors will say anything to get the job. You need to be as objective as possible when selecting a contractor for your project. Good contractors usually have strong portfolios and positive reviews, but they may charge more for their services. You also need to look for a contractor who has the skills and experience needed to do a good job on your project. If you're still not sure which freelancer you should choose, ask several contractors how they would approach your problem. If a contractor seems to have the skills you need but refuses to produce work samples, feel free to find someone else.

If you're working with a contractor for the first time, consider starting with a small project to help you evaluate the vendor's style and quality before you pay for a more complex task.

3. Assign a task

Once you find a contractor, provide clear instructions on how you want the task done. Make your expectations clear; don't assume the contractor knows everything. If possible, create a statement of work that includes the project requirements, cost, timeline, payment schedule, and a list of deliverables.

4. Monitor the process

Once you start working with a contractor, you have to monitor their work to make sure the project stays on track. If you pay a contractor an hourly rate on websites like Upwork.com, you can look at snapshots of contractors' computer screens while they're working.

Another way to monitor contractors is to ask them to send you parts of their work before you get the final deliverables. This helps you ensure each contractor is meeting your expectations, and it gives you time to request adjustments if the work contains any errors.

When working with contractors, don't try to micromanage your projects. Trying to manage every aspect of a project overwhelms contractors and saps their creativity.

5. Evaluate the results

When a contractor delivers your project, check to see whether it meets your expectations. In many cases, the contractor will need to make adjustments to ensure the project meets your requirements. Don't be afraid to ask for changes—a good contractor will be patient enough to make any adjustments that make sense.

You must follow all of these steps if you want to use outsourcing successfully. Depending on the project, there might be additional requirements to discuss with contractors before you let them start working. Set aside plenty of time to do research and get ready to work with your contractor.

Key Takeaway Points

- Outsourcing is essential because it allows business owners to get things done efficiently.

- The main advantage of outsourcing is to free up your time for important tasks that build your business' growth.

- Some beliefs can prevent you from outsourcing. Understanding and overcoming them are the keys to start getting the advantages from outsourcing.

- Learn the process of outsourcing and hone this skill so you can maximize the return on your investment.

Summing Up

"A real decision is measured by the fact that you've taken a new action. If there's no action, you haven't truly decided." —Tony Robbins

At this point, you've read every strategy in this book and learned how each one can help you increase your productivity. Let's review what we covered.

1. The mechanics of success: The first chapter starts by outlining the three principles successful people use. They are (1) think big, (2) go small, and (3) be consistent. You need to understand this formula for success before you attempt to learn new strategies for productivity. If you don't understand what it takes to succeed, you're likely to fall short on your journey. Keep this formula in mind, and you'll find it easier to appreciate your work process.

2. Identify your real priorities: All work is not created equal. You learned that only a few activities will contribute to the majority of your results. You need to spend most of your time on these activities if you want to be productive. In this chapter, you found a framework to help you identify your priorities.

3. Play to your strengths: When you play to your strengths, you tend to be more engaged in your work and produce better results. You learned that you shouldn't focus on your weakest areas because you will never be truly good at them. This chapter provided strategies to help you discover your strengths and capitalize on them. There were also tips on how to manage around your weaknesses so you can be more productive.

4. Create a simplified system: You learned a system to help you organize your work and free your mind for more important tasks. The purpose of this system is to collect ideas, projects, and random thoughts and turn them into actionable items. Once you have a system in place, you'll be confident that every project is on track. This chapter also provided a variety of tools to keep your system running smoothly.

5. How to work at your fullest capacity: Getting enthusiastic is the key to high productivity. There's no point in working if you don't commit to each project and focus on it to the best of your ability. You learned effective ways to eliminate distractions and to stop multitasking. You also found ways to take control of your energy level and shift your internal state so you're ready to work.

6. Seven habits of highly productive people: The majority of your success will come from maintaining consistent habits. It's important to develop habits that support your success and help you stay productive. It's also important to drop the bad habits that inhibit your success. In this chapter were the seven habits of highly productive people.

7. How to develop new habits: To successfully form new habits, you need to understand how habits form. In this section, there were five steps for developing new habits and making significant changes in your life.

8. Overcome procrastination: Procrastination is the biggest obstacle to productivity and success. There are three main reasons people procrastinate: they lack confidence, they lack energy, and/or they have psychological issues. The tips and techniques in this chapter should help you overcome each problem.

9. Get more done by outsourcing: You can't be a lone wolf if you want to be truly productive. You need to outsource some tasks to free up your time for the tasks that generate profit and grow your business. You learned how to overcome the attitudes that prevent you from outsourcing and the strategies to ensure you get the highest possible return on your investment when hiring a contractor.

There you have it: a complete set of strategies to help you become a highly productive person. Even though this book is shorter than some books on the same topic, it's packed with essential content that will help you transform your life.

7-Day Action Guide

If you've read the entire book and completed all the exercises, congratulations! You're making huge progress on the road to becoming a master of productivity. However, the concepts in this book are meaningless if you don't put them into action. When you start implementing all the tools and techniques, you're going to develop a whole new perspective about your work. You'll see significant results in the following days and months.

To make it easy for you to put the concepts in this book to work, a worksheet complements this book for your use. Inside this worksheet, you'll walk through a step-by-step process to complete the exercises in this book in seven days.

Here's the link you can download the action guide:

http://www.chaiwatspace.com/worksheet

Don't fall into the trap of thinking you need to read more books and articles on productivity before you take action. You already know what you need to do to be more productive. It's simply a matter of taking action right now instead of trying to gain more knowledge.

Notes